Contents

Some words are shown in bold, **like this**.
You can find out what they mean by looking
in the glossary on page 31.

Who was Captain Scott?

In 1911, two groups of men set off to reach the **South Pole** for the first time. Roald Amundsen arrived there first, but Robert Falcon Scott's heroic adventure and death will always be remembered.

This photograph shows Captain Scott standing next to his sledge.

The South Pole is the most **southerly** place in the world. It is roughly in the middle of the continent of **Antarctica**. At the South Pole it is dark all the time in winter and light all summer.

Antarctica

Antarctica is so cold that there are no trees anywhere on the continent.

Early years

Robert Falcon Scott was born near Plymouth in Devon on the 6th of June 1868. He had a brother and four sisters. At school, Robert studied hard. He wanted to join the **navy** like two of his uncles.

Robert grew up in a big house in the country.

After school, Robert joined the British Royal Navy. Learning to sail ships was hard work, but Robert did well. He became Captain Scott when he was chosen to lead **expeditions** to the **Antarctic** in 1901 and 1910.

The unknown Antarctic

The **Antarctic** is the coldest place on Earth. It is almost completely covered with very thick ice and is surrounded by a cold ocean. Penguins and seals live there.

Penguins are one of the few animals that live in Antarctica.

Captain Scott wanted to be the first person to reach the **South Pole**. He also wanted to study the Antarctic. Nobody knew much about **Antarctica** 100 years ago.

Today there are buildings at the South Pole, but 100 years ago no one had ever been there!

Sailing to the Antarctic

On his first trip to the **Antarctic**, in 1901, Captain Scott and his crew travelled in a wooden sailing ship called the *Discovery*. The *Discovery* had to be big enough to carry everything the 47 people and 23 dogs needed.

The *Discovery* had to be very strong to sail through sea ice.

Captain Scott's second ship, the *Terra Nova*, had a special **stable** for the **expedition** ponies.

Captain Scott had to take food, fuel, medicine, and other supplies for life in the Antarctic with him. He also took scientific equipment, books, and even a piano! On his second trip, in 1910, he took ponies and motor sledges as well.

Life in the Antarctic

When the **expedition** members arrived in the **Antarctic**, they had to build a hut to live in. They also needed somewhere for the animals to stay.

The hut was warm and snug against the strong wind and cold Antarctic night.

Can you see some of the things that Captain Scott took with him to the Antarctic?

As leader of the expedition, Captain Scott had his own area in the hut. It was here that he planned the exploration of the Antarctic and the team's scientific work.

These photos show the bunk beds and kitchen in Captain Scott's **Antarctic** hut.

Other members of the **expedition** slept in bunk beds. Captain Scott's men used boxes of supplies to make walls inside the hut. There was also a kitchen where meals were prepared.

Everyone stayed inside during the long winter months, keeping warm around the stove. When they finished their work, they wrote diaries, painted pictures, and sang songs.

Here, two of Captain Scott's men are cooking food for the ponies and keeping warm at the same time!

Travelling on the ice

When spring came, Captain Scott and his men practised pulling their sledges using skis, **snowshoes**, dogs, and ponies. They also had motor sledges on the second trip, but the sledges broke down in the very cold weather.

The motor sledges ran on tracks, similar to a tank.

When they were ready, Captain Scott and his men set out for the **South Pole**. They pulled sledges loaded with tents, food, and fuel, helped by ponies and dogs. Travelling over the soft snow was very hard work.

The sledges were very heavy. Each one weighed more than 100 kg – that's like pulling more than 100 big bags of sugar!

Reaching the South Pole

On his first **expedition**, Captain Scott had walked closer to the **South Pole** than anyone else at that time. He eventually reached the South Pole on the 17th of January 1912, on his second trip.

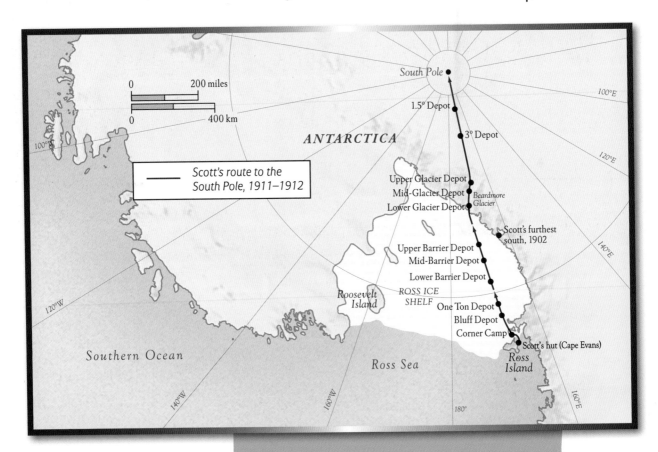

Depots of food were left for the return trip.

Doctor Wilson.   Captain Scott.   Petty Officer Evans.   Captain Oates.   Lieut: Bowers.

A number of men helped carry supplies on the trip, but only five went all the way to the South Pole.

It took Captain Scott and his four **companions** 78 days to travel the 1,450 kilometres from their hut to the South Pole. When they got there, they were cold, hungry, and very tired.

Captain Scott and his men had wanted to be the first people to reach the **South Pole**. However, when they got there, they were disappointed to find out that the Norwegian explorer, Roald Amundsen, had got there a month before them.

Amundsen's team left a tent and letters for Captain Scott at the South Pole.

Next spring, other members of Captain Scott's team built a **cairn** of snow over the place where he died.

The journey back from the South Pole was very long and the cold days of autumn were coming. Captain Scott and his four **companions** never arrived back at their hut. They died of cold and lack of food on their way back.

Remembering Captain Scott

When the news came back to Britain that Captain Scott and his men had reached the **South Pole**, their story became famous. The Scott Polar Research Institute in Cambridge was set up to remember their bravery and achievements in the cold **Antarctic**.

This is the building of the Scott Polar Research Institute in Cambridge.

The Scott Polar Research Institute's museum has scientific displays about the Antarctic and the **ice sheet** that covers it. You can also see letters, diaries, and other objects from Captain Scott's **expeditions** there.

These goggles, gloves, and **balaclava** were worn by Captain Scott and his men in the Antarctic.

Paintings and photographs

We can find out more about Captain Scott, his **companions**, and the **Antarctic** by looking at paintings and photographs. Edward Wilson was a scientist and artist who went on the **South Pole** journey with Captain Scott.

In this photograph, Edward Wilson can be seen working on a painting in the expedition hut.

The large painting shows people camping in a **blizzard**. Wilson also liked to paint pictures of penguins.

Expedition members like Wilson had plenty of time to paint, especially in the winter when they had to stay in the hut because it was dark all the time and also very cold. These are two of his paintings.

A photographer, Herbert Ponting, also went with Captain Scott to the **Antarctic**. He took many photographs of the trip. Here is a photograph of the members of Captain Scott's **expedition**.

Can you see the hats, gloves, and boots that Captain Scott and his men used to keep out the cold?

Ponting's photographs showed people back in Britain what the Antarctic was like. The photograph on the right shows an ice cave with the ship *Terra Nova* in the background.

The smaller photograph shows Herbert Ponting standing next to his camera.

The Antarctic today

People still explore the **Antarctic** today.
Some are trying to learn more about the land
and weather, and the animals that live there.
Others are trying to set records.

In 1994, Liv Arnesen became the first woman to
ski alone and unsupported to the South Pole.

Today's Antarctic scientists are able to use modern equipment to help them with their work.

Captain Scott's team thought that scientific discoveries were just as important as reaching the **South Pole**. Today, scientists study ice in **Antarctica** to learn about Earth's **climate**. Their discoveries may help us protect the Earth in the future.

Captain Scott timeline

6 June 1868   Robert Falcon Scott is born

July 1881   Robert joins the **navy**

July 1901   Captain Scott leads his first British **Antarctic Expedition** on the *Discovery*

January 1902   Captain Scott crosses the Southern Ocean and sees **Antarctica** for the first time

December 1902   Captain Scott sets the record for going the furthest south

September 1908   Robert Scott marries Kathleen Bruce

June 1910   Captain Scott leaves Britain on his second polar journey, aboard the *Terra Nova*

1 November 1911   Captain Scott sets out from his hut at Cape Evans towards the **South Pole**

17 January 1912   Captain Scott reaches the South Pole

29 March 1912   The last entry is made in Captain Scott's diary, making it the probable date of his death

Glossary

Antarctic south polar region

Antarctica very cold continent located around the South Pole

balaclava knitted hat that covers your head and neck with a hole for your eyes

blizzard storm with wind and blowing snow

cairn man-made heap or pile of snow or stones

climate the usual weather in a place

companion someone who spends a lot of time with another person

depot place where supplies are stored

expedition journey that is taken by a person or group of people to little known places

ice sheet thick ice that covers a large area

navy part of a country's armed forces that work at sea

snowshoe platform shaped like a tennis racket that can be attached to a shoe. Snowshoes are used to help people walk across snow without sinking.

South Pole place that is as far south as you can go

southerly in the direction of the south

stable building animals are kept in

Find out more

Places to visit

The Polar Museum, Scott Polar Research Institute
University of Cambridge, Cambridge, CB2 1ER
www.spri.cam.ac.uk
This museum is full of items from Captain Scott's expeditions along with paintings, photographs, and other materials on polar exploration and science.

Discovery Point Museum
Discovery Quay, Dundee, DD1 4XA
www.rrsdiscovery.com
Visit the ship that Captain Scott used for his first Antarctic expedition.

Index

For activity ideas and teaching notes visit: www.raintreepublishers.co.uk/content/DOWNLOAD